Fix your Financial crisis

Slavica Bogdanov

OTHER BOOKS BY THE SAME AUTHOR

Be Free!
Conversations with Angels 1 and 2
101 Easy Ways to save Time Every Day
101 Easy Ways to Save Money Every Day
101 Easy Ways to Sell More Every Day
Escape Once and for All
Road Block Busters
The Art of Instant Happiness
Boost your Brain Power
7 Secrets to Reprogram your Brain
Amel Santorin: sailing in the Greek Islands

ISBN:148025147x
ISBN-13:978-1480251472

Prosperity is the possibility to do what you want to do when you want to do it. » Raymond Charles Baker.

Slavica Bogdanov

CONTENTS

"I believe that the power to make money is a gift from God." John D. Rockefeller

INTRODUCTION

Do you feel like you cannot make ends meet? Do you want to have more money? Want to get out of debt? Do you feel like the recession has decided to move in to your home for good? Yes? Well, I have been there once, and know how it feels. Do you want to be richer? Do you want to rapidly increase your wealth or simply become a millionaire? Do you want to find a better job or, finally, do what you really want to do in life and earn a living from it?

There are a few methods I have used that can definitely help you. I have also researched and read many autobiographies of successful individuals to understand what made them so.

Before we start, we need to determine the reasons why you want to have more or owe less? Do you think that having more money will bring more happiness? Sure you do, everyone wants to be happy. Most of us know that money does not bring you more happiness; some say it makes unhappiness easier to live with. Seriously, if you are looking for money for the wrong reasons, you might never really acquire more or if you do, you may not be happy at all.

What is certain is that money cannot be an end. It can be used as a means to getting somewhere better or helping others. Acquiring wealth for the sole purpose of being wealthy usually attracts more misfortunes. It is best to determine exactly what you think and feel about money. How you perceive the accumulation of money. This first step is very important for you to take to get rapidly on the right track.

When I did the exercise at first, I thought about all I wanted to buy with the money. Slowly, I understood that I really needed nothing of it all. I realized that, what I truly wanted was more time. Eventually, I knew that money would buy me time to do what I loved doing. Then, the thought occurred that, if I was paid to do what I loved doing the most, I would get much more value out of the time and the money. When you reach that kind of wheel of fortune and joy then you almost forget about becoming rich, or richer.

> "If your goal is to become financially secure, you'll attain it...But if your motive is to make money to spend money on the good life...you're never gonna make it."
> Millionaire next door

I have a friend of mine that is always talking about people that have become rich. Almost every week, he wants to start a new business that someone else started and that made him successful. I always ask if he is sure he will feel passion and enthusiasm when copying someone else's enterprise. Faced with the obvious look of uncertainty in his eyes, I know his method will mean almost instant failure. The only way to have more money is to create it while doing something that brings you joy simply because you will need that passion and enthusiasm to keep you going when times are tougher. Mostly, you need to enjoy life while you are getting to your goal. The road to success must be as pleasant as the destination.

Work and money are obviously linked tightly in most of our minds. As you may already know, it is not the amount of work that determines the amount of money you can or should have. The sentence "work hard for your money" is obsolete. You can actually work much less and earn much more. In reality, the less you spend time working, the more time you have to think of yet other ways to generate more money. We need to keep in mind that we also have the ability to create ways where money actually works for us.

Work is also related to money in a dramatic way when resentment fills our daily routine. You go to work backwards. You hate what you do all day. I found it interesting how people are always so stressed out on the roads and become even infuriated, they so much want to arrive on time at a job they can't stand. I would try to get there as late as possible if I hated what I was doing. Actually, no, I would quit that job. Life is too short.

I am certain that we all still have a child inside our soul. Somewhat of a temperamental kid that wants his toy immediately, that wants to play and definitely does not want to work. I have noticed that sometimes I was controlled by that kid. I used to go buy an item I absolutely did not need and would not even need in the next month. I realized that that child had needs and wanted to be satisfied at least once in a while and the more I made him happy the more he cooperated in my success. For example, when I renovated houses, I promised myself I would take a terrific trip (since I love to travel) somewhere on the sea. I basically bribed the child in me. I don't think I would have the strength or the determination to continue working as hard without it. Every time the child in me wanted to complain and take a long break, I would think of the luck I had of not having a 9 to 5 office job (that I couldn't stand) and that in a very short time, I would be out of this construction site and off to paradise. I think we all need to satisfy that part of us, reward us, congratulate us.

What happens when you do a job that you hate? Well, you frustrate the kid in you. For example, I can spend hours writing without even noticing it, because I love it. I forget the time and even to eat. The child in me is happy because the job I am performing is like a game and kids love games. When I worked in an office, even if I was doing my job passionately, I was not totally satisfied, and I did feel frustrated many times. When you don't like what you are doing, you upset that child and you feel stressed out and unhappy. What happens then unconsciously, you try to bride the kid in you. I don't know about you but when I was a kid, I was bribed all the time by my folks. "If you are nice, you will get that gift at Christmas (isn't there even a Christmas song that goes like "you better watch out, you better not cry..."); "if you eat all that is in your plate, you can have desert"; "if you don't stop, you won't get". I heard it all the time and I am sure you must have too since I still hear it all the time around me in the stores. Therefore, when we do something we hate, we bribe the kid in us. How? We go on a shopping spree. A total waste of time and energy.

How long do you feel happy when you buy yourself something-anything, a pair of socks, a beautiful sweater that just happens to be on sale when you were passing by that store? Shopping to have as a short term boost of happiness can be addictive and disastrous on a financial level. You may end up in terrible debts with loads of useless purchases that only created a five minute sensation of joy. The worst part is that, by doing so, you build yourself a high security jail cell. You become a slave, literally. You work at something you hate to get money to buy stuff you don't really like so you forget you work in a place you hate to pay for the stuff... well, you understand the vicious endless circle. You can break free from it.

Getting out of debt

To create more wealth, we need to get rid of bad debt. I define bad debt as any debt that is holding you back from advancing such as credit card debts, student loans, car loans. I call good debt, the kind of debt you use to create more wealth. Such debt can be understood in terms of mortgages for example.

In an upcoming book on real estate and mortgages; I speak more thoroughly of ways to get rid of debt. I will share with you here some basic ways to help you out quickly and then we can focus on more ways for you to acquire more money.

Facing debt is like facing any of our hurtful defaults. A lot of us have played the ostrich game and hid our head in the sand not to see this problem until we cannot escape any longer because it has become an enormous monster. In turn, the debt leads to increased stress; which in turn leads to many physical, personal and interpersonal problems.

Debt is an obstacle to wealth building because you spend a lot of money on interest rates. You also spend a lot of energy thinking about the bills. With the principle of visualization and focus that I talked about in the "14 keys", what ever you place a lot of attention on tends to acquire more importance and grow. Therefore, if you place your attention on late bills, chances are you will get more bills. It is very important to step out of that vicious circle.

One of the best ways to get out of personal credit card debt is to refinance your home, if you have one. The monthly payments on your new mortgage can be increased by very little, yet you might be able to get rid of the high credit card interest rates. If you are able to get rid of the debt by refinancing understand the luck you have and don't get back into debt again. As a mortgage agent, I saw many times people refinancing their homes to get rid of their credit cards debts and getting right back in the same problems only a few months later: overspending, miscalculating, and using credit as if it was free money.

If you do not have a home to refinance or cannot get money out of it, then you need to rethink your financial world. You can use the same method as if you wanted to lose weight. Write down where you spend the money (do this for at least a week). Start immediately. Use any paper handy and write what you have spent on today (include the little details such as coffee and this E-book). Carry a mini note pad in your purse or attached to your wallet to force you to remember to write it all down.

Once you have a list of all you spent money on that week, you need to start cutting out what is absolutely not necessary. A coffee a day is over $600 a year. A trio in a fast food restaurant is not only bad for you but, if you do it every day, it cost you over $2000 a year and you probably will have gained a few pounds of fat. What about restaurant take outs? Or, that new shirt you just had to buy since it was on sale. Buy three get one free. You probably never intended to get one item and you are buying three for the freebie. Did you get extra make-up because they were offering a gift with every purchase? Do you throw away a lot of food? Evaluate your spending habits and you will be shocked by the amount of wasted money. In order for you not to be traumatized by a drastic change of spending behavior, allow yourself a monthly gift (not an Armani suit of course), small one, pay cash for it.

Lay down the credit card bills in front of you and start calling the lenders. If you ask for it and insist, they are willing very often to bring down the interest rate. That, of course, if you have been paying at least the minimum monthly payments on time. I lowered mine from 24 to 11%. When I told my mother about this, she couldn't believe it. We went to one of the banks she had a credit card with and I asked the person in charge to change her card to get one with a smaller interest rate. She had a 19.5% interest and I knew the bank offered cards at 10%. I was shocked by the reply I received. The employee told me that it was a really bad idea because she wouldn't get the same travel insurance coverage. I explained that we didn't need the insurance coverage. Then, still trying to discourage us, she went on about something else we were getting with the card. Again, I expressed the fact that my mother really didn't care about all the fluff; she just wanted the lower rate. The discussion went on for a few minutes as she was probably testing my patience. Eventually, my patience left the bank and the employee had to change the card rate. The funniest thing about the adventure is that the woman ended up saying that she was disappointed my mother wanted the other card since it was meant for people who were poor and didn't pay on time. "Fantastic", I replied and added "I bet the poor people's card doesn't have an annual fee either". I was right. In the other bank, my mother went from a 19,5% to 5,6% interest rate in a matter of minutes!

In the financial world exists a rule called "the 72 rule" that calculates how much time it will take to double your financial investment. It states that when you divide 72 by your interest rate, you get the number of years the amount of your investment will double. For example, if I invest $50,000 in a fund that brings in a rate of 10% (first I would jump for joy because those don't seem to exist anymore); I will see my investment double to $100,000 in a little over 7 years (72 divided by 10 equals 7.2 years). The same maths applies to credit cards interest. If you owe $5,000 to a credit company and have an interest rate of 20%; you will owe $10,000 to that company in 3 1/2 years. You probably won't notice this amount since you probably will be making the required minimal payments on your credit card which usually pay off only the interest on the card.

To get out of debt, the first step is to stop using your credit cards until you pay them all off totally. So, take them out of your wallet right away and store them in a safe place. And, I don't want to hear the usual excuse of "I might need it in case of emergency". Most people I have heard say usually encounter only emergencies of purchasing useless things. Then, look at your credit card bills and decide which one you will pay completely off first. Usually, it is best to start with the one that has the less owing amount and the greatest interest rate. Then, use a portion of the money you have decided to use to get out of debt towards that credit card first and put a much greater chunk of money on that one. Use the rest of the money to pay a little over the minimum payment on the others. Why do this? If you divide equally what you want to spend to pay off your credit cards, you see very little change every month later which can be very disappointing and discouraging.

Slavica Bogdanov

If you see at least one owing amount diminishing rapidly, it will encourage you.

I would greatly advise you to get rid of store credit cards and never get them again. I know we are all lured by the "don't pay a cent for the next eighteen months" kind of deal. Don't be fooled by it. The reason is that you risk a very bad surprise if you don't repay it on time (like a accumulated 30% interest rate on the balance) Also, if you want to buy a house in the short to middle term (or refinance the one you have), you need to stay away from store credit cards as they have a very negative impact on your credit rating.

Also, and most importantly, we start a non logical way of thinking when we accept to acquire a store credit card and not pay for twelve months. If we buy with the intention of paying in twelve months, we need to make sure we have the money in twelve months; which we cannot be sure of since we can't predict the future. The only way to be absolutely certain we will have the money in twelve months is if we already have it in a savings' account. If we have it now then we don't need the credit card in the first place. The "don't pay a cent events" is one of the greatest money making marketing techniques and scams I have seen. It beats the "buy two and get the third one free", it is above the "the more you buy, the more you save" kind of slogan. It is the ultimate since you will purchase an item on sale and pay for it at a higher cost when you are done. Let's say, you are thrilled in acquiring that sofa at $1,800 instead of $2,000; with the offer of not paying for it for a year. During that year, the joy of buying the sofa will have been long gone and you might even start wondering what gotten into you in making that silly purchase in the first place. Then, you forget about the bill and one day, when the year has passed, you realize you will have to pay $2,340 (which is the balance added to the cumulative interest rate of 30%).

I still need to advise you that you should have

credit cards, if you want to purchase a big ticket item like a home, one day. You need to not use them until you pay them off but don't cancel them all. I would keep two of the ones that offer the lowest interest rate. I know it seems totally contradictory. Once you have tamed the spending beast in you, you will need to use you credit cards once in a while (very wisely!!) and pay off the total of what you have spent every month. How to do this? Intelligently is the rule. Spend only what you can repay, know it by creating a budget.

Pay your bills on time. It will help you on the subconscious level to acquire more self esteem and respect. Paying on time is like keeping a promise. Always pay more then the minimal payment on a credit card if you can't pay it all. Remember that if you can't pay it all the next months, it means the "purchasing beast" is back in you. Therefore, once again, stop using them and start the process of repaying them all. If you notice it at the beginning, and change immediately your behavior, you will be on the right track faster. Also, before spending on futile purchase, pay what is necessary on your cards. I recently received a call from one of my tenants. He lost his job a little after the first of the month and asked to have more time to pay his rent, until his unemployment insurance would kick in. I asked him what he had done with his last pay check instead of paying the rent with it. He answered that he had given the money to his wife in order to buy Christmas presents. I was flabbergasted. I have nothing against the spirit of giving especially at Christmas time. What I find most unbelievable is to think of buying gifts before thinking of maintaining a roof over your head. This is an example obviously not to be followed.

A key you can use to help is visualization. Pick a credit card bill, erase the amount and write $0 owing instead. Focus on getting to that 0. Every evening before you go to bed, visualize a debt free life (I know you will feel happy as you do this). Repeat a positive affirmation morning, night and every time you can:

"This debt shall go away. My subconscious mind will find ways for me to achieve a debt free life. I thank God in helping me achieve this goal."

Other keys that you can use to get out of debt are determination (don't give up), faith, positivism (even if it sounds very difficult). You need to be focused on your goal. Start immediately. Get your bills out, gather your family to explain that some changes are to occur (and no, you won't be buying your teenage daughter, the bran new super cool jeans she just saw on sale and that she must have or she will throw a fit).

I _____solemnly declare that as of this day, I will work my way out of debt. I will remain positive and determined to succeed. I will not use my credit cards until I am free of debt.

Creating a budget

How many of us truly know how much we spend every month? How many of us are actually scared to find out? The truth is that if you don't seriously work on understanding your spending habits, calculating a budget for yourself and obeying it; you have very little chance of becoming financially free as you will always be confronted with an unexpected expenditure which will put you behind.

Most of us hate the perspective of creating a budget. We feel that it will restrain us from enjoying life. We think budgets in negative terms. Actually, creating a budget frees you from being controlled by expenditures. When you create your budget, you can see where you are going, and you can make a plan and take the reins of your finances. If you want to get somewhere you need to know where you are going. By creating a budget, you can find true financial freedom.

How to create a budget? First you need to list all expenses you have, precisely. You can find a table to fill below. Calculate your monthly fixed expenses (mortgage, rent, insurance, car payments, property taxes,...). Subtract those from your net income and also the variable expenses (fuel, food, bills,...). If you are not sure about upcoming variable spending you can: one, determine a reasonable budget (for food and fuel) and two pick the last bill you have and add some extra money for the calculation purposes (so you have less bad surprises). You are left with an amount of spendable income. Before you do anything with it, you need to remove a portion to place it in a savings account (having automatic withdrawals set in place is the best way to save). You need to put some money aside for unforeseen events and some money aside for pleasure and education. A percentage of your net income should be devoted to donations to charity organizations (when you feel you can be happy about giving to others, don't just force yourself since it will defy the purpose). This exercise should be repeated every month until you do it automatically. If, after all of that, you have still money left; save more of it. If you have a negative result when you have done this exercise, you need to go on a financial diet. Set your self a specific goal on how much you want to save each month and work your way towards it.

Your   monthly   Household   income is:_____

Remove   immediately   10%   for saving:_____

Total   income   left is:_____

Necessary spending	Amount	Change
Home rent or mortgage		
Home insurance		
Property taxes		
Water and sewage fees		
Car loan or payments		
Car insurance		
Health insurance		
Energy bills		
Children Education		
Total		

Secondary spending	Amount	Change
Telephone bill		
Credit card payments		
Food inside the house		
Fuel or transportation		
Total		

Unnecessary spending	Amount	Change
Eating out		
Clothes		
Going out		
Club or community fees		
Other		
Total		

Extra spending	Amount	Change
Charity		
Saving		
Investing		
Knowledge		
Fitness		
Gifts		
Total		

If you cannot make ends meet, you need to cut your expenses. Cut as much of it as you need to end up with a positive budget. You can start with the unnecessary spending, move your way up to secondary spending. From eating out, decide to cook; from buying tons of groceries and have lots to through out, make a definite list of meals you will prepare that week and then go pick exactly what you need. Of course, try not to be too restrictive so you don't break your own promises. By following a budget that has specific goals, you will feel more in control of your financial life; you will regain self confidence and will be wealthier.

As you have notices, there is a table called extra spending. Those items should become slowly part of the first, necessary table in your budget; and should replace the unnecessary spending if you don't have money for both.

Your financial freedom consists of the choice you are responsible of taking. You are in control of your finances. Your job does not pay you enough? Start by spending less. Your kids are always asking you for money and you can't say "no"? You are in control, not your kids. Teach them the value of money by making an example. When at the store, take the time to think: "Do I really need this? Do I need it now? Am I going to let myself be influenced by a sale once again? Can I afford it?" On the other hand, you can calculate what is your net hourly wage and associate the purchase with the work that it took to generate the income to buy it. A pair of pants is no longer a number with a sales tag attached to it but 3 hours of work. It might influence your purchase frenzies.

Choose a method, any method. The importance is to be determined, disciplined and wise. The less you will be a slave to compulsory buying, the more free you will feel; you will regain your power and your self esteem. Living well below your means and controlling your spending are the best ways to get richer and stay rich.

> "Penny-pinching is the
> opposite of being
> wasteful. I have never
> liked waste, whether it's
> time, effort or money. I
> think I inherited this
> attitude from my parents,
> who were careful with
> everything, particularly
> money. I still don't like to
> overspend for anything,
> and I will always take the
> time to compare prices,
> whether I'm buying a car
> or a toothpaste." Donald
> Trump. Think like a
> Billionaire.

I would have one last suggestion for changing your buying habits. Carry cash around and store away the plastic. Have a good amount of money in your pocket, whatever you consider to be a lot whether it is $100 or $1,000 or $10,000 doesn't matter. Spend very little of it. Don't use your debit card. Bank cards have totally separated us from the rationalization of spending. When you use plastic, it is much more difficult to keep your budget balanced unless the account from where the debits are placed is totally separate from all the others and is only a spending account. When you use money, you have a better sense of how much you are spending. You can withdraw the amount you are able and willing to spend monthly and use only that cash.

I have to admit being pretty lucky in the sense that I never have been a shopaholic. I actually don't like to shop very much so I am protected a bit. Nevertheless, I found a way to refrain myself from buying even more. First, when I do go shop for a piece of clothing, for example, I will write down exactly what I want to buy. It is a rule that we learned when doing our groceries: buy when your stomach is full, make a list so you don't purchase food you didn't plan on bringing home, or junk food that you want to stay away from. So, I write down, for instance, that I want a dress and the kind I would like. Secondly, unless it is absolutely necessary (which is rarely the case) like needing a bran new dress for a wedding to which you were invited at the last minute (it is really rarely the case); I always shop against the current. Meaning that I always buy out of the season or at the end of the season. I dislike being too trendy and prefer dressing up in more classical types of outfits (the trend lasts longer). I linked a long time ago the "being in" fashion with the "being in" jail. Therefore, I can purchase items for the next year and get them at a great price. If I do want a piece of clothing that is fashionable (and I know the trend won't last long) then I buy it in, what I call, the "get and chuck" stores. Those are the places that sell lower quality clothes for very cheap. I know I will wear it for a short while and give it away so I don't spend much on it.

Before I go shop, I look through my closet to see what I already have bought in the past. Some people tend to forget the treasures they have, hidden in the back of their closets and keep on buying more. Then, I will spend a lot more time in the store than necessary. If I find an item that resembles what I had in mind to purchase, I will carry it with me for a while. I will role play as if I had already bought it. From there, I calculate my level of happiness. Am I extremely happy or just satisfied a little? Is it exactly what I wanted or am I just settling for less? Is the price really good and affordable or am I just blinded by my liking the product? Do I think it will be on sale if it isn't already? I hate purchasing stuff at top dollar, choose to wait for it to come down in price. I even prefer not to find the item again and not buy it than to pay full price for it. Sometimes, I will return to the same store three times to check on my item before I buy it. Last but not least, when I purchase my dream dress and bring it home, I will wait a day or two to see if I am still happy with it. If I am not, I will return it to the store for a refund. Try this method, you will notice that your spending on unnecessary items will drop considerably.

Slavica Bogdanov

Making more money

One way to have more money is obviously to spend less. Have you noticed how often we tend to increase our spending as we increase our earnings? Millionaires are renowned for their frugality and it is probably the frugality that helped them build some of the wealth. The other way to have more money is obviously to earn more. Where do we start to earn more?

Ask for a raise? Why not? If you don't, it means you don't think you deserve one, therefore you don't deserve one. Your thoughts control your actions; your present actions control your future.

How to deserve earning more? Make a list of your achievements and successes. Accumulate all client letters or benefits you have generated with your work for your employer. Show your enthusiasm and passion. Give more service to your client, do better, and know more. Take courses in improving yourself and the knowledge you have about what you do. Still no raise? Change bosses. Just kidding or I am?

You want to make more money, start thinking that you can, you want it and deserve it. The "how you will get there" will come to you in time. Change your opinion about money. Listen to your thoughts. Making money is a mental state, not a physical one. To acquire wealth, you need to get rid of your negative ideas about money. The "money doesn't grow on trees", "you need to work hard to make money", "life is tough", "you don't deserve to be rich", "you'll never make that much", "who do you think you are", "it is not Christian to seek for wealth", "money is dirty" and more of the same. Does it happen that you pass in front of as store and a little voice inside your head says "I'll never be able to afford this"? Do you listen to yourself speak? Not yet? Well now is the time. Write all of the negative thoughts you have about money, all of them, quickly without thinking, write all that your subconscious is giving to you. It can be as simple as "I have no idea how I can make it", "I'll never be able to..." and more.

Once you are done, you need to replace all what you wrote by positive statements. Those will become your weapons against negativity. I am suggesting a few I am using and I would encourage you to write some of your own. As soon as a negative thought comes up, let it come out and then reply and repeat.

- I have enough money to buy anything I want (don't go on a buying frenzy nevertheless)
- I deserve to be rich and prosper
- Wealthy people can be nice and generous
- There is no limit to how much the Universe can offer me

- I am a millionaire already
- The Universe is abundant and offers unlimited wealth and I am ready to receive it
- God is good and loves us, therefore he wants to rejoice in wealth, health and love.

Are you afraid to be rich? In your subconscious mind, do you associate wealth with hard work and less time for family and friends? Do you think that if you become outrageously wealthy you won't be able to hang out with the same friends? I have noticed that in a lot of movies, rich people seem very serious, tired, stressed out, negative or nasty, and look like they have chosen money over everything else. As soon as you remove those images from your mind, you will realize that you can have both money and family, money and free time, money and laughter. I noticed that you can find many romantic movies that end well and are very helpful in visualizing a great relationship. There aren't many movies about making a lot of money without much effort and, mostly, legally. How come?

I have a friend that told me he felt greedy by wanting more; as if it was egoistical and negative to want more money. I told him about Bugatti. The latest fastest car in the world sold for a little over $2.4 million dollars recently. The Bugatti company released soon after a Bugatti Hermes edition which was sold for over $2.7 million. When asked why they had built a more expensive and luxurious version, the answer was simply "because some people just want more". It kind of convinced my friend that his wanting a little more money couldn't really be considered as greed when we compare it to the abundance of the Universe. Also, It is when we think of lack, that we fear of lack and believe that our wanting something is taking it away from others. That is not the case. We all deserve better and we all can have it.

By changing the way you think about money,

your attitude will change in receiving it. Have faith that the world is abundant and there is enough money for everyone.

Is time really money? If you think so, then start saving time. Time is money when you know how to spend time efficiently. For instance you should always start by giving time to what generates the most income and not waste time on worthless details. Learn to delegate the details so you have more time to generate more wealth.

"The key is not to prioritize what's on your schedule, but to schedule your priorities." Stephen Covey

According to the Pareto principle, we can deduce that 20% of your time can be invested in what creates 80% of your fortune. Disorganized, you may spend 80% of your time on what would generate 20% of your income. See the difference? Determine what steps are most important in order to gain financial freedom or accumulate more wealth and do those first and foremost. Calculate the energy you spend compared to the financial reward you gain out of it. Focus on spending less energy to gain more money.

Keep your goals in mind but focus on your immediate responsibilities. Don't cling on to the results. Detach yourself from the outcome. Have faith that you will get there and that your subconscious mind will find ways for you to get there. What you try to hold on to the most is actually pushed away. Use time in your favor. Take some time each week, alone and in silence preferably and let your mind think about how you could make more money. Eventually, you will notice new ideas coming to you, sometimes really profitable ones.

You want to earn more? Visualize how much

more do you want to earn? Do you have a number in mind? When I started to change my mentality, I wrote a number down. It was $122,000 that I wanted to have in my bank account by the end of the year. That was three years ago. The year after that, I got a bit more ambitious and wrote down $500,000. A few months ago, I wrote that I wanted to earn a million a year. There is no limit to what you can have. There is no impossible number. You are the one that sets your own limits in life. You have nothing to lose in wanting a large sum of money. The worst think that can happen is that you get a little less than the large sum of money. I suggest you write that number and place it in an obvious place where you will see it often.

Write it here. How much are you worth?_____

How much do you think you can earn next year?_____

Write your goal:

I_____ intend to
earn_____ or more by the end of
_____or earlier.

I wrote this declaration a post-it that I have stuck on my mirror and also in my wallet:

"I am happily and honestly earning a million a year. I do this by writing books which are intended to increase the level of collective awareness and help people become greater and happier. I achieve this by acquiring more real estate properties that I fix in order to offer better quality housing. By earning this income, I can rebuild destroyed Monasteries and give the gift of knowledge by building more schools throughout the world".

I would suggest you do the same. Until you

come up with your declaration, you will probably write a few and then, change them as you grow. Imagine a way that you can help a lot of people, find your inspiring statement and write it below. I am certain that you can only achieve riches by doing something that you love doing and helping other.

I_____, will make _____a year before the end of _____by helping people with my _____(you can name abilities or products).

Read you statement morning, evening and every chance you get. Be thankful for what you already have and yet ask for more. Believe you deserve it. Keep a positive attitude no matter what. Act as if you have already achieved financial freedom. Feel the happiness of having the income you dream of having. Read autobiographies of people who are wealthy. Join a high end club and socialize with the kind of people you want to become. Take that sport convertible car you dream of for a test drive. Feel the joy as if it was already yours.

If you want to earn more, you might want to consider learning more. Knowledge brings wealth. If you know your profession better you will be one step in front of your competition. If you learn about managing your wealth, chances are you will. Take the time to develop your knowledge about money. Expand your awareness so that you can grow richer. Devote some money into education so that you are always learning. Wealthy people dedicate time to better themselves constantly. Read books about wealth, go to seminars that speak of sub-subjects concerning money. You may want to learn ways to pay fewer taxes, increase residual income, and invest in the stock market. Experts are always paid more. Become an expert at what you do. To do that, you need the passion in order to have the energy to spend the time. Find a mentor, someone that is wealthy, to help you go through the steps. Mentors are much accessible than you think.

Slavica Bogdanov

Don't be cheap with generosity

"Like a river, money
must keep flowing,
otherwise it begins to
stagnate, to clog, to
suffocate and strangle its
very own life force."
Deepak Chopra

I witnessed a very disturbing incident a few weeks ago and share it with you so we can learn a positive lesson from it. I was waiting a few cars behind a vehicle stopped at a red light. An individual had approached the car to ask for some money. The beggar was insulted and replied to the driver who opened violently the car door which hit the beggar. Before anyone who was shocked by this cruel act of violence could do anything, the light changed to green and the assaulter vanished. I felt really sad for the beggar. I could not believe the violence I had just witnessed. Another day, a friend of mine was asked for money by a beggar on the street and refused vehemently without even looking at the man. We are all people. We are all equal in the fact that we are all the same, related in some spiritual way. I ask what feels better; assaulting a beggar, refusing to share; or just giving a few coins? You have the answer. I prefer to give. I even prepare change in advance now so I have something to give. When I don't, I, at least, look at the person in the eyes so that they feel human as they should. We ignore beggars, like we ignore old people. We think that by ignoring them, we have less chances of getting there. By giving, you feel the joy; you become empowered because you become your own hero.

A universal rule stipulates that the more you give, the more you receive.

"Many people in poverty consciousness think that money shrinks when you give it away (100%-

10%=90%). The enlightened Millionaire knows that giving money actually expands in the spiritual dimension (100%X10%=1000%). Tithing is a money multiplier, not a money subtracter. It expands, multiplies, and adds value to all that you do". Robert Allen. One minute millionaire.

Therefore, make sure to use 10% of your net income to give to a charitable organization. In the case of the book you are reading, 10% of all proceeds will be directed towards a non-for-profit organization.

Slavica Bogdanov

From rich to millionaire

The number of zeros you place after the "1" in your definition of wealth is irrelevant. It is your belief of what you truly deserve that will define what you will earn. The difference between a five or a six digit figure is just an extra number. You have to start believing it to get there. Faith is the first step to riches.

List below twenty things that you would do with a million dollars:

1_____	11_____
2_____	12_____
3_____	13_____
4_____	14_____
5_____	15_____

6_____   16_____

7_____   17_____

8_____   18_____

9_____   19_____

10_____   20_____

You will probably have a hard time listing twenty ideas at first, but the first one that should come to mind is that you will donate $100,000 to a charity. What would a million change in your life? Make a list of the benefits. Is it that important for you and why?

How to earn a million dollars? Mr. Steinberg (that had built an empire on franchising grocery stores) answered when asked the question: "It is very easy, buy a million socks at a dollar a pair and sell them for two dollars". Seriously, there are a lot of ways. It is not the how that really matters; it is your own programmed thoughts that count. Once you change those, you will see the opportunities arise. Once they do, jump on them. Visualize the result and let go of it.

To become a millionaire does not necessarily mean that you have a million dollars in a bank account. What it means is that your net worth is of a million dollars. You calculate your net worth by adding the worth of all you possess (car, house, bonds, savings…) and subtracting all that you owe (credit card debt, loans, mortgages…). The result is your net worth. It is much more relevant, if you want to become a millionaire, to calculate your net worth. Start immediately. At least it will give you an idea of how close or far you are.

You can increase that net worth by having more of the positive or by getting rid of the negative. You start by deliberately deciding that you want to earn a million dollars. You are free to set the goals you chose.

I saw this very funny scene in the movie "Duplicity" when a multimillionaire complains about the fact that bowling is uninteresting because you have a ceiling of only a possible 300 points. "What is next?, he asks". The same rule applies to your profession. What is the salary ceiling at your work? Can you make a million doing what you do? If your wish is becoming a millionaire and your job has no chance to offer you that possibility, than you need to decide what you value more. What is your freedom worth? Millionaires chose both freedom and money. Also, keep in mind that you still need to work in a field you are passionate about.

I struggled a long time with the concept of working for someone else. I could not bare the thought that I was offering my time, my energy, my ideas and my life as such a cheap price. I felt my freedom was worth much more than my pay. I spent my days in anguish always imagining what I could be doing with my time instead of sitting in an office. And I was amongst the lucky ones since most of my previous life (before I became semi-retired) was in sales where I was paid according to my efforts. Yet, it never felt like I was paid enough.

Millionaires are mostly self-employed. They have started their own company and work for themselves. They prefer to earn money according to their efforts rather than be paid an hourly wage. You can develop some of their qualities and imitate those: perseverance, positive thinking, generosity, energetic, disciplined, expert in his field, intuitive, wise, organized, determined, creative, ambitious, strong, fearless (or at least acting in spite of fear), bold, fast, self confident and open minded. The millionaire evaluates and plans but decides fast and well. Once a decision is made, it is not reconsidered, it is acted upon. Once an action is finished, it is never regretted.

Millionaires have money working for them instead of working for the money. How, they invest in creating and developing sources of residual income. A residual income is basically income that comes regularly without you having to invest effort or much time into making it. There are different sources of residual income and you might want to learn more about the one that you feel the most comfortable with. Amongst others, there are real estate investments; stocks, bonds purchases, network marketing, internet, and opening your own company.

Real estate investments offer you multiple ways to increase your income. You are forced to save by paying into your mortgage. Also, the property's value usually increasing with time, your net worth increases as well. Thirdly, if you have income properties, your tenants' rent become a source of income. Investment in bonds and stocks can also bring you residual income as you gain from the interest. Internet can become a source as well as you can create a web site that will sell for you day and night.

Millionaires believe they deserve to be millionaires. They believe in abundance. They know what they want and do what it takes to get it. They know that the future is not affected by the past but only by present actions so they focus on what they do in the present and do it well. They save money to better reinvest it. They are frugal. If happy, they know that their happiness is not caused by their wealth. They love what they do and they work passionately and enthusiastically regardless of the money earned. They surround themselves with a team of experts to whom they delegate with trust. They hang around millionaires. They are grateful for what they have. They face reality pro-actively and respond to problems by searching for solutions. Knowing where they are going, they become great leaders. They are not afraid of falling because they have mastered the art of getting up so they understand that failure is just another expression of opportunity and amongst others an opportunity to learn and grow. They spend more time creating the world they want to live in than watching it. Life does not just happen to them, they make life happen.

The worst you can be faced with if you want to become a millionaire is to become only close to a millionaire. The best that can happen is that you become a billionaire. One way or another, if you do not know what you want to become, you have better chances of facing mediocrity and accepting it as destiny. Since you are here, it means you have chosen wealth. By doing so, you have accepted your responsibility in acquiring it. If you can do it, you must do it. If you can't do it, it means you don't know how. Learn how.

You can start by behaving as if you already were a millionaire, visualize and feel like one. Believe that you deserve the millions and let go of the future. Meditate and use silence to quietly plant your intention into your subconscious mind and send the energy into the Universe. Persevere and keep working towards your goal by setting yourself smaller reachable daily goals. Close yourself up to any negativity that surrounds you and only use the positive energy you have to advance. Become an expert in your field, be open to ideas, and look for opportunities by focusing on the present. Organize time efficiently and manage what the monies you already have wisely. Save both time and money to reinvest them into more beneficial channels.

I have done it and so can you. It takes patience, determination, faith, time, detachment, openness to intuition and observation of coincidences. Remember that the walls you have build around your prison come from your mind only. For the chains you have locked around your feet, you have the keys. You are a magician. You start creating magic when you start believing you can. Ask for more and you will receive more. Be sure of it.

Slavica Bogdanov

Transforming work into play

Prosperity is the possibility to do what you want to do when you want to do it. » Raymond Charles Baker.

Since we spend a minimum of a third of our lives on the work place, it is important to like what you work at. If you don't, the job definitely becomes a prison and you are sentenced until you retire if you have the means to do so. I heard it many times: "I still have ten years to go", as if we were speaking from inside a cell. It is totally up to you to change for the best. It is your life after all and it is worth it.

The least I can say is that I had had many many different jobs. I started working when I was about eight, helping my parents at their pastry shop. For about ten years, I served the clients, and after a while even dealt with some of the accounting. I was a cashier in a gas station during my University years and also a receptionist at Cinar Animation which was really interesting since I could see the making of cartoon animation. It fascinated me. I also was a book critic on different radio shows.

For some time, I worked closely with Mr. Tilden when Tilden Rent-A-Car was one of the fastest growing most promising car rental companies in the world. I liked him a lot. He was like a father to me. I am sure he acted like a father or a grandfather with all his employees. Tilden, the company, felt like a giant family. The president had great management skills, knew how to listen and to direct without making anyone feel like they were merely employees but more as if they directly contributed to the success of Tilden and, at the same time, their own. When he died, and his kids took over, I left. Tilden the company had died with his leader. Any future manager could greatly learn from him.

Later, I worked in Paris for the biggest producer of French printed media in the world, for those that care about Elle Magazine, Photo and many more. It was fascinating to be so close to the fashion industry, the French way. For those of you who have seen the movie "The Devil Wears Prada", you will understand what I mean. The assistant daily life in that movie, actually, looked very close to mine in those days. I loved the fact that we would receive so many goodies from all the brands: lip sticks, food, scarves just to name a few. What I didn't like was the rigorous inflexibility of the hierarchy. I was faced with the discouraging feeling that one could never climb the stairs of ambition two by two but only one by one and slowly. I am of a very ambitious nature and would rather climb stairs three by three. The reality was very different. On top of it, salaries varied depending on each department chief's mood and there was no rational between hours worked, pay or size of responsibility. There was a lingering dissatisfied feeling amongst the office clerks because we felt we were openly rejected by the pseudo high class business.

For a few months, I worked as a flight attendant. Thrilling experience where I learned once more the benefits of remaining calm at all times. After a couple of months of training, each new flight attendant was to take a first flight before earning her or his wings, which consists of the pin that bears your name. My first flight was to take me from Montreal to Vancouver. I was very existed not only because I was going to fly as a stewardess for the first time but because I had a long flight which I found was much more fun because you have time to chat with the others and eat more. Anyway, we reached our destination and, as we were waiting for the plane to refuel and the passengers to be seated; the pilot, while going through his check list, noticed that one of the door light indicators was showing open when in fact the door was closed. The passengers were already seated and starting to show signs of impatience. The captain was refusing to sign off the log book. If he had, it would mean that all was functioning perfectly with the plane. He was hesitant because he didn't feel reassured that the door was, in fact, well locked, and that the illuminated button could actually be showing a malfunctioning mechanism which could lead to more serious dangers once we would take off. The maintenance crew, after spending over half an hour checking the door, convinced the pilot that the light indicator was defective, not the door; pressuring him to reluctantly sign the log book. So we departed. As a new flight attendant, we are closer in our memory to all the different security lessons we have learned, and I felt edgy. None the less, I had the intention to serve the pop drinks with a smile. I had just started to pour the first drink when I sensed a hand on my shoulder. My spine felt a chill and cold sweat rushed down my neck. I turned around and saw the eyes of the chief flight attendant. I knew it was serious. She didn't have to say a word. I secured my serving tray and went to the front of the plane.

There, I saw the first class flight attendant holding the door handle with both hands. She looked as if all her strength was used to hold it down. I stared at her in disbelief when she explained that, as she was about to serve coffee, in the corner of her eye, she noticed a motion and her reflexes prompted her to jump on whatever was moving. The handle had been dislodged from the secured position on the malfunctioning door and the door could open. The pilot had been right, it was too late now. He had already started the maneuverings to bring the plane back. Very dissatisfied passengers had heard the announcement evidently being unaware of the dangers we were facing. Our role was to remain totally calm.

We went through the rows to make sure all had put

their seat belts back on and as I started my tour in the first class, I noticed a gentleman obviously in a state of advanced anger nervousness speaking on his cell phone. I calmly asked him to turn it off. He looked at me straight in the eyes, managing his anger, he congratulated me on keeping such a straight face and then, advised me he was one of the chief supervisors of the maintenance crew at the airport we just had left and informed by the control tower, he was fully aware of what we could expect. Still, I told him to hang up. We strolled between the seats as if we were taking a pleasant walk in the park. My heart was beating to a breaking point and I hid my fear behind a genuine smiling face.

I was seated for landing next to the flight attendant who was still clinging to the door handle. She had chosen not to let go of it and face death first if ever something else would go wrong. For those that are unfamiliar with the process, there is a very high risk in landing again after flying for a shorter time than originally intended. Since we were not allowed to dump our fuel over the city (fuel in a plane is contained in the wings), we were full, the wings bent with the weight. That is unimportant except in a landing situation when the wings can touch the ground and a very small contact can create an irreparable disaster. Since I am writing this down, it is obvious that there was no plane crash involved and we all safely landed. The flight attendant who hung on to the door was taken in under medical supervision since her arms were totally bruised, some veins had literally popped from the effort.

I always thought I was lucky in life; therefore I handle fear pretty well. Nevertheless, I did pray hard on our way back, asking for past mistakes forgiveness and promising I would do something of great value to the world in return for my life. I hope I keep my promise. In the meantime, the plane was checked by maintenance and a new pilot signed the log book. A new flight crew was brought on board but they were short of one so I flew back on that same plane that scared the hell out of me the first time. I was ressured by the probability calculations that led me to believe it was almost impossible to relive the same event twice in a day. Luckily I didn't and I earned my wings.

I did a lot of odd jobs. I used to be very good in sales. At one point, I worked as a Director at a town's council, marketing division (I was the division). I took at heart to help an animal sanctuary that was in desperate needs of funds to be able to build a better fence around the wild animals that were scaring the farmers in the neighborhood. I imagined a way to get them the amount they needed by selling holes. Holes they would need to drill to have their fence posts in place. I thought that only the craziest idea could create enough publicity to help them out. Well, it worked. They build their fence and I had the pleasure to play with baby cougars.

For fifteen years, I worked in sales, mostly advertising. I sold space; which is similar to selling holes. I was one of the top sales persons, selling emptiness, space to be filled with ads. I loved doing it. It was like a game for me. I was so tenacious that clients would inevitably say yes at one point or another. Management told me that if I couldn't sell something, then the product was at fault. Since I had also worked in a survey company, I was almost completely immune to clients' rejection. A "no" only meant that I should try harder. The only part that I really disliked in sales is that I felt I was worth much more than my pay, and that I was creating a lot of wealth for my employer only.

In the last job I had, working for someone else, I liked my boss, I liked the people I worked with; I just felt unsatisfied. I can't even say I hated my job. I enjoyed it. I felt like I wanted more out of life. I wanted more money, I wanted more time to write and paint, I wanted to retire early, I wanted to travel more, I wanted to buy beautiful things (cool cars especially). Before I found my true purpose, I wanted material things and, as well, felt like life should mean more than working every day creating wealth for someone else. I liked my job but I was not enthusiastic about it; I wasn't passionate about my work. I just lived or survived without feeling alive.

Are you like me? Maybe you just hate what you are doing every day. Why do you do it? No choice? There is always a choice, often one doesn't want to take the decision, but the choice is always there. No money? You don't need money to be happy in your job. You are scared to change in the context of the current economic situation? There is never a bad time. You have responsibilities and can't quit your job? Of course don't quit but change, look, study, evaluate and jump.

Do you like your job or do you consider it to be work? Do you separate work and play or do you feel work is play? I met numerous people that hate what they do. Yet they do it eight hours a day, five days a week. They complained to me and probably still complain to others. I was one of them.

People that like what they do, do it because they like what they do; no matter what amount of money they earn. I am sure that, as soon as you only do a job for money that is when it is time to change professions. If you would unexpectedly come across a large sum of money, would you still do what you are doing now? If your answer is that you would immediately quit your job, well it means that you should already think of a change. If Donald Trump still buys buildings, it is because he has so much fun doing it. If Celine Dion sings, it is because she loves it. If you don't love what you do, the money you will receive will never bring you satisfaction, nor will you make a fortune. In the previous section about finances, you read about the fact that, you can only make a fortune when you love what you do. It is the love that will give you the drive to do that no matter what happens. The passion and enthusiasm at work will give you the endurance, perseverance and determination you need in order to be successful.

You don't need to jump into the unknown blindfolded. The first step is to find out what you like doing. Name five aspects of your current profession you like:

1_____

2_____

3_____

4_____

5_____

Name five aspects of your current job you dislike:

1_____

2_____

3_____

4_____

5_____

Name five qualities or talents you have:

1_____

2_____

3_____

4_____

5_____

List what really matters to you

1_____

2_____

3_____

4_____

5_____

Is there anything that you currently do or that you would do that you would not care earning money for? Something you can do all day, all night; that feels more like a hobby than a job. Is there anything that you never get tired of doing and that, when you are doing it, time just flies? For me, it is writing or buying real estate or painting. For you, it might be different. Think about what you enjoyed doing as a kid, as well. What did you dream of becoming? What stopped you?

Last, but not least, think of the reasons why you believe you were put on this earth. This is probably the toughest one, yet crucial. I am certain that everyone on this planet has a role that is greater than his own self. Think of what your purpose is. Living without purpose feels like a meaningless life. We don't just get born, reproduce, create wealth for us or others, love and die. There is more and you feel it as soon as you understand your purpose. One way to discover it is by thinking of ways you can be of service to others. Mine, of course, is to free and empower the most amount of people by raising their level of self awareness. What is yours?

Finding what your dream job would look like can be a long journey. Yet, it is in that field you have more chances of becoming wealthier and live happier while you become wealthier. Sometimes, what we love to do is staring at us in the eye; we are just scared of admitting what it is. Why? Because we think we will never make a living out or if. Interestingly enough, we hear stories everyday of people that have switched either by choice or by force (after a lay out) to do what they loved and were inspired to find ways in doing it. You need honesty with yourself. You need to make an important choice: when you know what you want, are you ready to go get it? I believe, we have only one chance to make the best performance there is out of our life. We can be a class act and create an outstanding magical concert with our life or we can accept mediocrity. There is no middle ground. By the way, it is never too late.

Think of the day when you will be at the end of your life. Looking back at these years that are now only memories of the past, what do you want to think and feel? Do you want to stare at an empty theater where only desolation still lingers on? Do you want to be one of those people that talks about successes that have happened such a long time ago that they only reflect the uneventful recent past? Do you think you will be scared of dying because you will have wanted just one last chance to make it happen or will you die with a peaceful heart knowing that you have lived your life to the fullest? At the end of the road, there are no more excuses one can give, only the reflection of past actions. I want to think that you are strong, filled with willingness to achieve your dreams. Remember, that they will never be an ocean mankind cannot cross, and a moon mankind cannot reach when he sets his heart on it. What is

Slavica Bogdanov

the moon you want to reach, what is your most important goal?

By answering these few questions, you will be closer to understanding what kind of life and what kind of job you would see yourself in. If you would have the freedom not to have to work, would you still be willing to do that job for free. If the answer is a passionate "yes", then you found your dream job. Then you have no excuse in doing what you were meant to do. If your eyes don't light up as you enthusiastically speak of your profession, consider a change. The next question is how? How change? One first must not fear change. You must want to and decide to. Once and for all, choose to live life deliberately.

You love sailing but have no boat, and actually don't even know the least bit about maneuverings; you can't even tell your starboard from your port side?

76

The first key is knowledge. In everything you do, always search to excel, be better, expand with knowledge, become an expert. My motto is: "If you can do it, you must. If you can't do it, it means you don't know how. Find out how". Go to the library and pick up books about what you love doing. Take an evening course that gives you more knowledge. Register in an online chatting group. Find a professional association and participate in their meeting by introducing yourself to the people that do what you love. Ask questions; ask to have someone give you direction in how they became what you want. Inquire about the pitfalls of that profession so that you are not totally disappointed later on finding out that those aspects are falling exactly in the five criteria of things you cannot stand. People want to help. You just need to ask.

A little over a month ago, I searched for a mentor. A lot of reference books were speaking about the importance of having a mentor that would help you and motivate you;

someone already in the field with more experience. I wanted a writer that dealt in real estate successfully. Simple task? Then, I thought how difficult it would be to travel all the time to meet with Trump (why not? Isn't he the one that is always telling us to Think Big?). I really needed someone closer to me. Wishful thinking? Ask and you will receive? Well, the same day, I came across, by pure accident, the name of a successful author who dealt in real estate. He lives ten minutes away from my home and was nice enough to invite me for a chat. We keep contact.

The second key is faith. You have to be sure that impossible is only a word that we invent to lock us up in the jail of impossibility. I am absolutely confident that impossible doesn't exist. Everything is possible. If God or the Universe or some higher Spirit has put you on this Earth to do something specific for which you are meant to be, as soon as you start going in that direction, doors open and you meet people that will help you. This is true simply because you are moving in the general flow of the Universe. Working in a profession that goes against your nature is like swimming against the current. It is tiring, stressful, painful and eventually dangerous. By not doing what you are meant to do, by not trusting your capacity to succeed in the path you should follow; you are insulting the Universe and telling the higher Spirit that you have no trust He knows what He is doing.

Accepting to spend time in a job that you hate is accepting to enslave yourself by chaining your soul to fear, cowardness, mediocrity and eventually regrets. The truth is that a lot of us lie to ourselves and hide behind unlimited complaining and winning. I have been there. How do we lie? We want to think we give out our best when we only wait for the end of the day to arrive. We want to improve ourselves in our work place but don't have the energy since it is drained by the negativity building up as we force ourselves to work in place we dislike. We want to change jobs but are afraid to make a move. We don't want to take action and face the unknown so we linger in a job until the unknown comes smacking our faces when we get fired or have a nervous breakdown. "But it is not my fault", "how can I change in an economic recession?", "I will lose my seniority and my benefits" (I love that excuse the most, especially when the company decides to go bankrupted for a while or restructure and the benefits and pension plans suddenly have very little meaning), "I am responsible for my family and cannot take the risk". Excuses only impoverish the soul. You need to believe you deserve better and that you can achieve your goals. Trust in yourself will cement your road to success. You are the only one responsible for achieving success. In any case, you don't have to give up your day job right away just because you want a better life for yourself. A lot of people do both until they build their business enough to quit the job they dislike.

The third key is determination. Imagine you always dreamt of opening a Bed and Breakfast. You finally are there and the first tenants decide to wreck the room ad clog the toilet. Would you give up? Close shop? No matter what you intend to do, you will find difficulties. You got to keep on going. The love and passion you have for your work are the means by which you can overcome the obstacles you might come across. There is a story told by Napoleon Hill about a man in search for gold, who after many attempts, disappointed and discouraged, sold his tools and plot to another man who hit the gold mine 3 inches only from where his predecessor stopped. Perseverance only can bring you to your dream Job and help you succeed in it. If you do not persist, it means that you lack the faith of getting where you want to go. If you don't believe it, than you don't trust yourself and you don't trust the Universe. Evidently, you see where it amounts to. If you don't trust the Universe that means that you just gave him direction to let you go. Therefore you fail.

> "In the realm of ideas everything depends on enthusiasm... in the real world all rests on perseverance". Johann Wolfgang von Goethe

Apparently, it is always just before we become extremely successful that we encounter a great problem, one that seems unsolvable. I am sure it is a way for the Universe to test our courage, our faith and perseverance to make sure we are worthy of getting to our goal. I am also certain, it is a way for Spirits to give us more courage, endurance, intelligence and abilities we will need once we reach our goal so we are able to fulfill the responsibilities and tasks of our new role.

Picture yourself there. Imagine dressed up in the clothes you would wear at that job, acting as if you were there. Feel the joy of having obtained that employment. Surround yourself with people that are enthusiastic and positive about their jobs and stay away from the complainers. Repeat a positive affirmation morning and night about your future job, like: "I am so grateful to be doing exactly what I want, thank you God".

Don't just try it- Do it

I really liked watching *The Secret* as it did open a large door in my mind in terms of possibilities. I did take the time to spend doing nothing. I say that because I think it is an important piece of information I should share with you.

I wanted to follow all they were saying so I did write down a check to my name with the amount I wanted to earn. Then, I started repeating every day that I deserved and was ready to receive the amazing good fortune that would come to me against all odds. I wrote all I was grateful for. Basically I did what they said I should do. After a while, I started getting really worried since nothing major seemed to happen. I am sure today that all that I did during that time was somewhat beneficial since it must have moved the Universe somehow to see me sitting around all day saying to my self, my friends and the Universe that a great thing was going to happen, that I was ready to receive a large sum of money and that still I was grateful for whatever I had. The Universe probably looked upon my sorry soul and smiled. I am sure He has a great sense of humor.

On the exterior, it looked like I was doing nothing. Actually, I was doubling the mistakes: I was doing nothing and I didn't know what I wanted to do precisely. I realized that spending my days wishing for a great life was amazing but that I should also work for it and find what I wanted to work for. I felt like I had followed a perfect recipe and forgot to turn on the oven. Everything did start to unblock once I made a list of goals, priorities and moved my butt out of the sofa and into the real world.

By the way, wishing does not do it for you; you need to have an intention. The difference between the two is that intention gives you back the freedom of the responsibility to improve your life where as by wishing, you only give the power of the control of your destiny somewhere out there without really intending to get there.

Once I knew what I wanted, by writing down what my goals were and what my strongest personality characteristics were; I got a sense of direction. I know you can get it too. Once that was done, I needed to put everything into action and create my desired future. It took me only two years. I have not reached all of my goals, merely a few; but nevertheless, one thing is sure, when you start moving in the direction you want to go, the whole Universe seems to give you a helping hand. I reached the most important goal: semi-retiring early. What do you want in life?

Participate actively in your life

The doing it part is a crucial element. Doing it means to first find what you really want to do and then put the effort every day to reach that goal. Start at the finish line and work your way back to know what you need to do to get there. Be flexible because many different paths can lead you to your goals and, as you acquire experience, knowledge and understanding, you will find a shorter road to get to your dream job. When you decide what you want to do, start there and work your way backwards to get a sense of what you need to do in order to achieve your dream job. Then, make a daily activity list of what you should do regularly to achieve your goal. And, of course, do it.

For instance, when I realized that I wanted to write

no matter what, I knew I had to have enough residual income to be able to spend my time writing. I read about ways to obtain residual income. There are investments but I always was scared of trading stocks. I felt it was not for me, at that time. The reality is that I felt so stupid trying to understand stock exchange, I didn't trust myself in trusting someone else to do it for me. The second way to acquire residual income was through network marketing but I didn't feel the drive or the passion towards that method either. The third was real estate. Since I was dealing with mortgages, I thought it was an appropriate direction.

Easier said then done. I am soon to publish a book on the fabulous hidden world of real estate investing and what people should know before hand. I did leap into it dressed up only with courage, similar to jumping off a cliff hoping someone would hand me a parachute along my descent. I ended being very successful yet I learned the hard way, and still learning. Anyway, when I found out that I wanted to go into real estate, I read a few books on the different ways to do and doors started opening that led me towards having a few rental properties in a very short time.

I am certain that, somehow, once you know what you want and you invest efforts towards your goal, the Universe answers by giving you more chances to get there. Like in a cooking recipe where the temperature determines the speed of cooking; in finding a job and doing what you love, it is your commitment and daily efforts that determine the speed of the outcome.

If you think you deserve it, if you invest into daily sustained persevering efforts, you will get there. Remember when you do to become a mentor yourself and share your experience with someone who wants to find his true path in life as well.

Conclusion: think of your children

As I watched a speech by Cameron Herold about raising kids to be entrepreneurs, a flash of light came before my eyes. Wow, I thought! What a great idea! People that know me a bit know how passionate I feel about changing or revolutionizing the educational system. Watching Cameron, I understood more about the small entrepreneur that could not wait to get out there and so, how much that proves him right.

As a child, I used to always hang out at my parents pastry shop. Actually, at one point, they had four branches and, at the age of eleven, I was asked to semi-manage one of them. I never realized until recently how much that single little event affected me in never being really able to work for anyone but myself.

Interestingly enough, although my parents were entrepreneurs, all they wanted me to be was a professional. Any profession that would make them real proud: a lawyer, a psychologist, an engineer, a biologist, a physicist; name it. At first, my mom, as a small town immigrant would even dream of me working as a secretary. She used to buy me cheap polyester clothes so I would look the role. I hated it.

As an eleven year old, I was passionate about plenty of other things. Since I had an hourly wage for my semi-managing one of the pastry shops and for my semi-accounting of the business. (yes, I was a bit gifted and my parents required some of my services in finances and secretarial work). One thing I loved doing, was to paint. Another, reading, a lot. A third, puzzles; the more pieces the more thrilled I was. I would do all in my room, which became my playground. That is what I call the place I live in now, as well. A playground. I love with passion all I do so there are no "offices" accepted in my environment.

Slavica Bogdanov

Fourth thing I was really passionate about: I used to love building houses. I was about ten, eleven. The small amount of friends I had talked about their Barbies. I preferred building homes. I used to go to the hardware store below our apartment and purchase all I needed to build dream homes. The wood, of course. The paint, evidently. I used to save the wrapping of the Babybel cheese I ate to create dishes, cutlery, bottles. I always loved cheese and I can honestly say, I really ate Babybel only for the wax. That's how much I was passionate about building my homes. And for those that know how much I love cheese, they will understand how much of a sacrifice that was. I used soap to build bath tubs. I thought it was clever since you wouldn't need any soap. I used coffee stirring sticks to make outdoor fire escape stairs. I used straws to make handles. Anything was good enough.

I feel I was extremely lucky. My parents were so busy running their pastry that they didn't have the time to cut me off from my passion. I spent days and nights working on floor plans and designs on how I would build a home. I didn't have Internet or books on the subject, I had to go by my only very small experience in these small projects.

I was lucky because, if my parents had had more time to spend with me, they would have definitely convinced me to do something else. Instead, my room was my paradise. On my real days off (when I didn't have school and when it was too late for me to work at the pastry shop), I would bring all I loved doing in bed. I had books to read, and crayons to draw and paint for my oil paintings and puzzles to finish. Multi-task? The least we can say. I was doing it all while watching "beep beep", the coyote show.

I am lucky to have lived in those years. When Michael Jackson was a famous pop singer and I could listen and watch all I wanted on my almost new television set (that I had also bought with my small earnings). I am lucky that I lived then. Today, if I was the kid I used to be, and the parents I see a lot around me; I would have been given some bi-polar disease medication to stop me from just being.

As girls were playing Barbie, I was building houses to fit their needs. Since I was too shy to speak to any boy, I was photographing them instead, which led me to another passion: photography. Actually, I even got orders from other shy girls to take pictures for them. Like a teenage school paparazzi.

I was alone. Most of my life. Most of my childhood and teenage years. And I am grateful. I had very little people to tell me what not to do so I had the opportunity to develop a lot of different skills. I couldn't be bored and I was over active so I always searched for ways to please both sides of my brain.

I also did sell whatever I could to make a buck. Not necessarily because I needed to but because I had time on my hands and selling stuff was fun. It created more money to buy more wood therefore more homes.... In those days, fun kid television shows were either early in the morning (like 6 to 10 for the Warner Bros) or 6 pm (for the Muppet show special) or 8 PM (for family drama movies). That gave me a full twelve hour to go wild and do whatever my heart desired (when I was not at the cash working for my parents).

Twelve hours when you are an over active kid means: a couple of paint by numbers paintings done (I didn't know I could paint without the numbers then), a home developing project started, a few hours swimming at the pool (which sometimes would be a full day), reading a book (200 pages would easily be devoured in a couple of hours), homework (I was somewhat gifted so learning was even boring), and some television in the middle of it all. Oh, and I forgot to mention, I was a folklore dancer performer which meant 3-4 hours practice weekly and when shows would come around, 8 hours daily of very painful to bleeding stage practices that I would have not missed for the world. Being able to control our bodies in some difficult group formations and be artistic at the same time was worth all the bruises and indescribable physical sufferings; that's when a body is painfully pushed yet again and again beyond its boundaries.

Entrepreneur? Attention disorder? Bi-polar disease? Overly acting yet extremely silent? I don't know what I was. Possibly all of the above. I know what I have become. I was cleaning the toilet of one of the buildings I own and it hit me. I was happy. In the most unexpected moment of all. And I realized, I always loved the homes for my Barbies. And I thought how lucky I was to be doing all that I always loved doing all the time. I write, I read, I paint and own homes. Thank God my parents were too busy to see what I was doing because they would have probably stopped me blocked by their own negativity.

So, please think about it. A lot of people put a lot of kids on this planet so they can say they have kids and feel good about showing off at least one thing they succeeding in making right. Well, please think about it. If you put kids on the planet, then, take responsibility on giving them the best opportunities to be the best, not perfect but excellent. Before you give your child any medication that will calm you down, think about it twice. Kids need to expand, they need to run, they need to fly and think and feel passion and jump from one subject to the other. And maybe, as Cameron states that bi-polar disease is called the CEO disease; maybe your kid just needs to be let to conquer the world with his ever so powerful entrepreneurial skills.

Think of what you really want for your child. Do you want them to grow up a slave or a free man? Do you want them to be wealthy, healthy, happy? Give them the tools today so they don't have to read my books later.

Slavica Bogdanov

Slavica Bogdanov

Fix your Financial Crisis

Bibliography

Harv T. Eker, The Millionnaire Mind, HarperBusiness, 2005

Trump, Donald. Think Like a Billionaire. Published by Ballantine Books. 2005

Trump, Donald. How to get Rich. Published by Ballantine Books. 2005

Fisher, Marc. Le Millionnaire Paresseux followed by L'art d'être toujours en vacances, Édition un Monde Différent, 2006

Leroux, Patrick. Le Feu Sacré du Succès. Édition un Monde Différent, 2006

Allen, Robert G. and Hansen, Marc Victor. The One Minute Millionaire. Harmony Books. 2002.

Rubin, Ellie. 7 Rules for Getting There. Penguin

Vitale, Joe. The Attraction Factor: 5 Easy Steps for Creating Wealth (or anything else) From the Inside Out. John Wi

Canfield, Jack and Hansen, Mark Victor. The Aladin Factor. Published by Berkley Books. 1996

Stanley, Thomas J. and Danko, William D. The Millionaire Next Door. Published by Pocket Books. 1998

Canfield, Jack with Switzer, Janet. The Success Principles. Published by Harper Collins. 2007

Fisher, Marc. L'Apprenti Millionnaire. Published by Un Monde Différent. 2009.

Chopra, Deepak. The Spontaneous Fulfillment of Desire: Harnessing the Infinite Power of Coincidence. Published by Harmony Books. 2003

Slavica Bogdanov

Covey, Stephen R. The 7 Habits of Effective People. Published by Free Press. 2004

Canfield, Jack and Hansen, Marc Victor. Dare to Win. Published by Berkley Books. 1994

Hill, Napoleon. Your Magic Power to be Rich: Featuring Think and Grow Rich, The Magic Ladder to Success, The Master-Key to Riches. Published by Penguin Books. 2005

Robbins, Anthony. Awake the Giant Within. Published by Simon & Schuster. 1991

Sévigny, Daniel. Les Clefs du Secret. Published by Editions de Matagne. 2007.

Murphy, Dr. Joseph. Miracle Power for Infinite Riches. Published by Parker. 1972.

Fix your Financial Crisis

ABOUT THE AUTHOR

Author of a dozen books, Professional Speaker on Efficient Communication (CPEI, a powerful mix between Emotional Intelligence and Non-Violent communication), Time management and Law of Attraction. Expert Consultant who insures you Reach your Goals!

Currently working on her latest book: The simplified Law of Attraction. A method she created to help people reach their goals faster, with more success.

Born in Belgrade, raised in Paris, Slavica completed a Master's Degree in History of Communications at the University of Montreal. She worked mostly in medias such as radio and print.

For 15 years, she helped businesses improved their sales and portfolio. Top sales person at first, she quickly moved on to becoming a savvy business developer.

She also devoted time in non for profit organisation. She believes that being of service is her utter purpose in life. She wants to serve as many as possible in developing ways to have a better life.

In 1999, returning from France where she had spent 3 years, she created the Balkan Peace Movement with the intention to raise Canadian public awareness and to encourage governments in searching for peaceful solutions. She starts on her own but rapidly gathers 30 people, Soon, 20,000 people follow her belief in the main streets of Montreal to protest the bombing. Two months later, she was invited to sit in the Parliament in Ottawa and speak with Party opposition leaders. That gave her the absolute certainty that any human can achieve any goal with perseverance and determination.

For 3 years, in 2005, she is marketing manager in the Prince Edward County Chamber of Commerce in Ontario. She mostly worked to encourage funding for an animal sanctuary.
Her life was always oriented in wanting to inspire others and achieve goals that many thought impossible.

Author of "Be Free", "Sailing in the Greek Islands" and "Conversations with Angels I and II", public speaker, life coach, Slavica Bogdanov is also a corporate speaker with Top Speakers.

Having studied and practiced the methods taught by successful authors in personal development for many years, she combined many of the teachings both spiritual and pragmatic to create a powerful and garantied ways to help people reach their goal, in any area of life.
She offers services as a life success coach.
http://www.slavicabogdanov.com

NOTES:

_____
_____
_____
_____
_____
_____
_____
_____
_____
_____
_____
_____
_____
_____
_____
_____
_____
_____
_____
_____
_____
_____
_____
_____
_____
_____
_____
_____
_____

Fix your Financial Crisis

Slavica Bogdanov